GARDENS *of the*
HUDSON VALLEY

GARDENS *of the* HUDSON VALLEY

PHOTOGRAPHS BY STEVE GROSS AND SUSAN DALEY

TEXT BY SUSAN LOWRY AND NANCY BERNER

FOREWORD BY GREGORY LONG

THE MONACELLI PRESS

CONTENTS

FOREWORD

Gregory Long
The New York Botanical Garden

Since the seventeenth century, the Hudson River from New York harbor to the old Dutch city Albany has been known as a brilliant inland waterway promoting commerce and industry. Since the eighteenth century, its banks have provided the setting for aristocratic houses and estates. And since the nineteenth century, the indigenous school of painting that grew up in the river valley has celebrated the beauty of the American continent. For all of these reasons, the Hudson takes its place among the world's most significant rivers—the Nile, the Ganges, the Danube, the Thames, and the river valley is famous here and abroad for its contributions to American life and culture.

And now, thanks to the photographs and essays of the four New Yorkers who have created this book, the Hudson River Valley can be understood as a living museum of American domestic garden design. This is because a two-hundred-year history of the American pleasure garden is illustrated, is revealed really, in the gardens here assembled. All of the plants of North America cannot be here—there are no palm or desert gardens, of course—but this is a fulsome survey of the styles that American landscape designers have created and promulgated from the early 1800s until today.

Beginning in the 1830s, there are gardens in the grand estate style, notably the Vanderbilt Mansion; in the picturesque taste, represented by Montgomery Place; and in the mid-Victorian gardenesque style seen at Locust Grove. And there are special versions of picturesque landscape gardens from the later nineteenth century—the painterly, sublime garden of Olana and the "tycoon picturesque" of Lyndhurst.

In the early twentieth century, American designers made gardens in the Colonial Revival taste, and these are represented by Bellefield and the later sections of Clermont. In the 1920s and 1930s designers invented the American "garden room," exemplified here by additions to the older garden at Montgomery Place. And, delightfully, there was "1920s eclectic international chic," wonderfully illustrated by Lisburne Grange. Mid-twentieth-century style can be understood in the small and sedate estate layout created for Boscobel. At the same moment, but at other extreme, the garden at Manitoga is informal and naturalistic, almost "back-to-nature." Illustrating garden styles in our generation, many gardens are represented, including the alpine garden and botanical collection at Stonecrop; the contemporary farm and garden of Amy Goldman, aptly described as a *ferme ornée*; and the postmodern layout at Tailings.

What a tour this is through the evolution of the American garden! And the wonderful thing is that most of these historic gardens are open to the public and maintained as galleries in a great open-air museum of American garden design. It is to be hoped that New York State and the private organizations that own these (now public) gardens and the museum houses they accompany, will stay true to their missions and preserve, maintain, and interpret these historic places far into the future. Earlier generations of families, preservation activists, non-profits, and State officials have saved these houses and gardens for us to visit and enjoy, and our generation also has its responsibility to these cultural resources.

So read on. Learn about American political and social history; learn about plants—from cannas to conifers; and come to appreciate this pantheon of American garden designers—from Andrew Jackson Downing to Frederick Church to Beatrix Farrand to Russell Wright. And plan a few excursions to these important places to be inspired by the sweep of the American landscape and to absorb our garden history at its best.

Spring 2010

INTRODUCTION

There is no part of the Union where the taste in Landscape Gardening
is so far advanced, as on the middle portion of the Hudson.

— Alexander Jackson Downing

This selection of gardens, chosen and sensitively interpreted by photographers Susan Daley and Steve Gross, evokes the grace and grandeur of the Hudson River landscape and underscores the central role the Hudson Valley played in the birth of an American garden tradition. Individually, each garden is a visual treat; together, they illuminate an often-overlooked aspect of our cultural legacy.

There are a number of reasons for the development of a garden culture in the Hudson Valley in the nineteenth century. By the early 1800s, there was a class of landowner with the means and the sophistication to think of landscape gardening as an art. The early Dutch, and then the British, had made a practice of assigning huge land patents in the Hudson Valley to wealthy individuals willing to develop the land, and their descendants formed a landowning class that populated the banks of the Hudson. By far the most influential and prolific family in the mid-Hudson was the Livingstons—the descendants of one branch of the family built thirty-six estates between 1742 and the 1840s.

In the early history of America, the Hudson River, navigable 150 miles up to Albany, was the super-highway of its time, permitting the relatively easy movement of people and goods between New York, Albany, and the territories beyond. Landowners often supplemented agricultural revenues with income from business dealings in New York or Albany, easily reachable by sloop and, after 1807, by steamboat. The splendid scenery, which included wooded shores, interspersed with sweeping lawns of riverfront estates, as well as thrilling mountain scenery, sparked the nation's first tourist industry, attracting many European as well as American travelers. It also inspired the young painter Thomas Cole and other artists, including his student Frederic Edwin Church, to record the majestic scenery, evoking an authentic American spirit through landscape painting.

As the country's intellectual life quickened, the quest to identify a truly American culture became a widespread intellectual preoccupation that often centered on America's relationship with its magnificent landscapes. No one was more focused on the development of an American garden tradition than the nurseryman, garden writer, and theoretician Andrew Jackson Downing of the Hudson Valley town of Newburgh. He was the most influential writer on gardens and domestic architecture of antebellum America, and the most popular "taste maker" of his era. He was also an early, eloquent supporter of the idea that public parks could extend the moral and spiritual, as well as physical, benefits of nature to the entire population, especially in the expanding, crowded cities. Both Calvert Vaux, who was briefly Downing's partner in his design firm, and Frederick Law Olmsted, credited Downing with the early dissemination of ideas that culminated in the creation of New York City's Central Park.

Influenced by the English garden writer John Claudius Loudon, Downing had studied the history of landscape design and especially the English Romantic movement, which he termed "the modern style," as opposed to gardens based on classical French or Italian tradition. His wide circle of friends included the architect A. J. Davis, with whom he collaborated on a number of projects. In books and articles, Downing sought to translate terms that had been applied to British landscapes to an American context, explaining for his readers the Sublime—natural landscapes so intense that they literally transport the viewer to a higher plane and something beyond the realm of a landscape gardener; the Beautiful—landscapes of rounded shapes, broad lawns, and groups of graceful trees, which characterized the Romantic landscapes of Capability Brown in England;

and the Picturesque—a rougher, wilder landscape with emphasis on pointy trees (conifers), rocky outcroppings, and roaring brooks. Downing felt the Picturesque was particularly suited to the American landscape with its vast wilderness not yet contained. The Gardenesque style, espoused by Loudon, which encouraged siting plants to their best advantage, was also an attractive concept to Downing, a deeply knowledgeable horticulturalist.

Using these terms, Downing argued for the "modern style," based on the British Romantic style but informed by democratic American values and American's unique relationship with nature. In his immensely popular *Treatise on the Theory and Practice of Landscape Gardening*, first published in 1841, he lays out his case for what he called "rural embellishment," and provides an overview of the gardening status quo in America, starting at the turn of the nineteenth century when, in his opinion, there were only a handful of estates worthy of note, most in the "ancient" (classical French) style. One of them was the first garden in this book, Clermont, the estate of Robert Livingston.

The Romantic landscape movement reached its apogee in England around 1800 but did not arrive in the United States until a quarter of a century later. Among the earliest American gardens in this style was the botanist and physician Dr. David Hosack's farm (later the Vanderbilt estate), designed in 1829 by André Parmentier, an influential Belgian nurseryman who had immigrated to Brooklyn and who was an early proponent of the *style Anglaise*. The Romantic picturesque style took hold in the Valley in estates like Montgomery Place and Blithewood and continued, after Downing's death in 1852, with gardens like Lyndhurst, under Ferdinand Mangold's direction, and Samuel Morse's Locust Grove.

Toward the end of the century, a noticeable shift in aesthetics occurred. The Hudson River School and its emphasis on the spiritual aspects of landscape painting faded, as did the concept that gardens needed to reflect the aspirations and philosophy of their ages. A wealthier and more self-confident America gave birth to a breed of unimaginably rich tycoons, some of whom gravitated to the Hudson Valley. Neo-Renaissance gardens of Beaux-Arts-trained architects appeared, often in conjunction with picturesque landscapes or layered over previously installed ones. At Blithewood, considered Downing's finest landscape,

the decaying A. J. Davis structures were replaced with a Georgian mansion and linked Italian garden. Similarly, a large Italian garden complex was inserted into a corner of Parmentier's masterpiece at the Vanderbilt estate. Probably the finest and certainly the best preserved Beaux-Arts garden in America is Kykuit, designed for John D. Rockefeller by William Welles Bosworth, its disciplined tastefulness reflecting the rather austere and serious outlook of its owner.

As the twentieth century progressed, a more supple and innovative approach to classical design emerged, which drew on an ever-widening variety of influences. Beatrix Farrand, a pioneer in so many ways, was steeped in the classical language of the Beaux-Arts and had also absorbed the plant-centered ideas of William Robinson and Gertrude Jekyll, as seen in her garden for the Newbolds at Bellefield. The focus on plants and the influence of Robinson and Jekyll resurface in two Livingston gardens, whose last chatelaines were both enthusiastic gardeners. Alice Livingston of Clermont and Violetta Delafield of Montgomery Place were absolute contemporaries and lived within ten miles of each other. Gifted gardeners and fierce rivals, both created wild gardens and enclosed Colonial Revival parterres. Their gardens, created in the 1920s and 1930s, mirrored fashionable garden trends of the times without disturbing the historic underpinnings of their estates. Another fine gardener, working essentially at the same time, was the very sophisticated Kitty Sloane, who developed Lisburne Grange as a green garden but sought help from Fletcher Steele, whose practice bridged Beaux-Arts traditions with a more modern sensibility. Unlike the seriousness of the gardens at Kykuit, Steele's classical references at Lisburne Grange are all made with a wink that indicates an awareness of changing times.

The last great innovator in this book is Russel Wright, who saw the beauty inherent in his scarred hillside of second growth forest in 1942, and teased it out over the next three decades. This respect and acknowledgement of the native landscape both harks back to the Hudson River School and Downing's championship of the American garden and prefigures our own preoccupation with native landscapes. It also enlarged our concept of garden, which at Manitoga is the designed native landscape.

The ten modern gardens featured here all relate in their own ways to the historic dimension of the region. Some are influenced by the historic architecture they modify, as at Hudson Bush Farm or Conrad Hanson's garden; some pay direct homage to a historic landscape, as the garden at River School Farm does to Olana; and some have similar sensibilities, as at Duncan and Julia Brine's garden in Pawling, which shares Russel Wright's respect for natural systems. Hosack Farm manages to be both an homage to the previous era and a quest to uncover the sublime in the indigenous Hudson Valley landscape. All these gardens build on the past, some in sophisticated and witty ways as at Tailings, some like Peter Bevacqua and Stephen King's mixed historical vocabulary used to create an intimate and pleasing place.

The common thread is the continuing presence of the gardeners. It is easy to imagine Dr. Hosack or Samuel Morse clipping grapes from the glasshouse for afternoon tea, or Violetta Delafield passing along a favorite plant. The rich life of these gardens can still be felt: the iron frames of the huge glasshouses at Lyndhurst remind us that every nineteenth-century estate of any size had glasshouses, most of which have not survived. Extensive carriage drives, which enabled owners to explore and enjoy nature and views at a comfortable pace, remain a pleasure of these historic landscapes. Their design was considered an art, and as disparate a pair of landowners as Frederic Church and Frederick Vanderbilt were united in their preoccupation with their lay out and maintenance.

The historic gardens presented here are living landscapes that continue to evolve, even as they are firmly rooted in the past. More and more, they are being considered important elements in the presentation and interpretation of historic estates. Each of the gardens in this book, public and private, tells a story about the people who made them and, collectively, they highlight the significant role of the Hudson Valley in the development of American landscape design. Daley and Gross's photographs give us the opportunity to reflect on the world beyond the frame, and to see the places where, as Downing once wrote, "nature and art are both so harmoniously combined to express grace and elegance."

CLERMONT

Germantown

For over two hundred years, Clermont was the Livingston family seat, and seven generations of this prominent Hudson Valley clan lived here. Standing on the western terrace of the manor today, the Hudson River is as vital a presence as it must have been to Robert Livingston in 1728, when he chose this spot on a gentle rise a stone's throw from the water. The river was their highway during the early years, a basis of great wealth, and, no doubt, a continuing source of beauty and enjoyment.

A second son, Robert Livingston, inherited thirteen thousand acres of the vast holdings of his father, the Lord of Livingston Manor, who owned a substantial portion of what are now Columbia and Dutchess Counties. Livingston built his family a Georgian manor house and named it Clermont, which comes from the French term for "clear mountain," a reference to the site's vast, unobstructed view of the Catskill Mountains across the river. His son Robert R., known as the Judge, inherited Clermont. He was often away, and when he was gone, his wife, the formidable Margaret Beekman Livingston, an heiress in her own right, ran the estate. She escaped the British in 1777 when they arrived to burn her house, and she returned shortly after they left to rebuild it exactly as it was before.

Clermont's most distinguished owner was Margaret Beekman Livingston's second child, Robert, whose many accomplishments included being the first chancellor of New York State, a signer of the Declaration of Independence, and the negotiator of the Louisiana Purchase. He was also the co-developer with Robert Fulton of the first steamboat, which stopped by the landing at Clermont on its inaugural voyage in 1807. In fact, though the ship was christened the *North River*, it has been called the *Clermont* by posterity.

The Chancellor, as he was known, was not only a statesman and businessman, but also a passionate farmer and agronomist who developed the vast estate surrounding Clermont into a model farm. He imported Merino sheep from France and pastured them on the long lawn, now sometimes called the sheep meadow, just south of the mansion. He also built himself a second house, called New Clermont, about three hundred yards from the original manor house. It burned down in 1909, but the ruins are still visible. Although there are no traces of Margaret's gardens on the east side of the house, we know that the long lilac walk, which originally linked Old Clermont to New Clermont, was installed sometime in the 1830s. Many of the oak and black locust on the property also date from that time.

The gardens and grounds at Clermont have been restored to the period of the 1930s and reflect the taste and skill of Alice Delafield Clarkson Livingston, wife of John Henry Livingston, the last private owner of the estate. A sculptor as well as a gifted gardener, she was strongly influenced by the popular Colonial Revival movement, and her aim for the gardens was to enhance the historic nature of the grounds. She insisted that the ruins of New Clermont be preserved, and she planted French lilac hybrids to augment the lilac walk. She loved planning gardens; the spring garden just south of the house with a view of the sheep meadow was a particular favorite. After returning from a stay abroad, Alice Livingston created the 60-by-30-foot walled garden and began developing the wilderness garden. With their informal disposition of shrubs and colorful perennials, both gardens show the influence of the English designer Gertrude Jekyll, but the walled garden also reflects the Colonial Revival style of the time, with its symmetrical parterres and low rock walls. In spring the garden beds are full of hellebores, lungwort, and thirty thousand bulbs, in the shade of several mature crabapples and magnolia.

During World War II, Alice Livingtson, by then a widow, left the house and moved into the gardener's cottage. While she continued to garden, she never really moved back, and in 1962 the house and property were transferred to the State of New York.

PETER BEVACQUA AND STEPHEN KING

Claverack

Intimately scaled and richly textured, this garden in the historic village of Claverack offers a series of carefully composed vignettes, in which the interplay of foliage against structure is animated by romantic details. Peter Bevacqua and Stephen King have been gardening here since 1989, cobbling together nine lots to form their two-acre corner plot. Except for a stylish crispness of detail, the exterior of the 1925 house gives no hint of the sophistication of the garden rooms behind, although at the entrance gate, the paperbark maple underplanted with lamb's ears and allium Schubertii certainly gives a strong hint.

The transition from street to garden is magical. Inside the gate, the dreamy modernity of Belgian designer Jacques Wirtz's carefully clipped hedging meets an English sensibility to plants. Partway along a curving grass path, a small bust of Dionysus (a reproduction of the original at the Capitoline Museum in Rome) peeks through the airy panicles of hydrangea 'Pink Diamond.' Further along, the eye is drawn to an unusual 'Dragon's Eye' variegated Japanese pine, one of many specimen plants that Bevacqua and King collected over the years and tucked into borders,

adding depth to each of the garden rooms. There is a maturity to this village garden, a patina of age that perhaps stems from the fact that the previous owners were gardeners too. The property came with a small Lord and Burnham greenhouse built in the 1950s and some established plantings, including a few of the bones of what has become the heart of the enterprise, the hedge garden.

A rectangular room of clipped yew and box, the hedge garden is full of allusions to other times and other places. The gravel paths and the green walls, with their slanting verticals and knife-sharp horizontals, echo traditional garden practice in France and Italy; the perennials that float cloudlike in the green room and the nepeta sprawling over the paths recall an idealized English border. Clipped boxwood balls and stone orbs reinforce the tension between circles and straight lines. The centerpiece is a cast-iron statue of the goddess Demeter, whose elegant form provides a satisfying focal point and completes the picture.

This is a garden that has evolved outward over time. A magnificent wisteria frames the back of the house, and the garden rooms nearby are tied closely to the architecture. The greenhouse, with its attached summerhouse, provides the opportunity for a deep and luxurious perennial border lining the access path; a pair of yews clipped into tiers marks either side of the entrance. A design studio and office becomes a spare, sophisticated backdrop for a formal gravel courtyard. Throughout, there is careful attention to detail: the planting is especially textured, like a complex tapestry rather than a painting of broad strokes. As the visitor moves outward, the smaller garden rooms give way to a looser landscape of mature trees and scope for more garden building.

HUDSON BUSH FARM

Claverack

I f Hendrick van Rensselaer, one of the powerful clan whose history is intertwined with that of the Hudson Valley, were brought back to earth today, he would surely appreciate the three acres of formal gardens that presently extend behind and beside the perfectly proportioned brick manor house he built in 1785. The gardens, which feel as if they had developed gradually over the entire lifespan of the house, have in fact evolved over the past thirty-five years, and the various elements, although informed by succeeding historical eras, are all remarkably compatible.

The first garden that Dr. Norman Posner and his longtime partner Charles A. Baker created after they bought Hudson Bush Farm in 1975 is the one immediately behind the graceful Georgian house. Enclosed by a weathered picket fence, the Anglo-Dutch-style garden is divided into parterres by a brick path and arranged using color wheel theory, one parterre featuring blue, indigo, and violet flowers; another, red, orange, and yellow. Nearby, an old smokehouse has been restored as a garden house. Overlooking the garden is a spacious open porch where the Boston ivy that clothes the house up to the second floor creeps in and covers the ceiling in the summer. Panels of white wisteria hang from suspended

ladders, and an enormous trumpet vine spills out from the footings. From the porch, there is a layered view over the parterre garden to the extensive lawn dotted with large shade trees and the farm fields beyond.

To the side of the house, massive clipped yews line a gravel path, the severity softened by plants that have seeded themselves along the base. The view is directed through this dark green alley to the bright field beyond. A white-painted Chippendale-style bench is inserted into the hedge, affording a long view of the lawn and flower gardens. The hedge garden intersects with a long, straight gravel walk, originally a farm road running from the main road to the fields, that is lined with waist-high yew hedges and a row of young pleached limes that were seedlings from a tree at the front of the house. On the other side of the gravel walk is a rock garden planted with perennials. The gravel walk ends at a summer house, formerly the icehouse for the property, which, with its nearby fish pond, set in a bower of hornbeams, makes a pleasing destination. Looking back across the lawn, with the trimmed hedges in the background, the eye is caught by a set of double red borders, filled with dahlias, cannas, and red-leaved foliage plants.

Although clearly influenced by an understanding of history and a respect for Hendrick van Rensselaer's house, Hudson Bush Farm today, while it is formally laid out, is a home, and not a "historic house." It has been the center of many public events, including an annual garden sale and exchange, and its gardens have made this incarnation of Hudson Bush Farm once again an important presence in the community.

GERALD MOORE AND JOYCE NEREAUX

Hudson

This garden lies a few miles south of the city of Hudson, on Mount Merino, a rounded, wooded hill with panoramic views of the Hudson River, named for the flocks of Merino sheep that Chancellor Livingston imported and bred in the early nineteenth century. Mount Merino was once a favorite subject of Hudson River School painters. The same qualities that attracted them attracted Gerald Moore and Joyce Nereaux when they chose this sloping hillside with its views of the river as their new home. Naturally, the glint of water is always part of the experience of their garden.

The garden's design is a result of the ongoing dialogue between Moore and Nereaux, who came from the worlds of publishing and art and have always shared a love for gardening. They attacked the place with great verve and taste, but they discovered that herds of hungry deer precluded extensive planting, so they confined their early efforts to areas close to the house, carefully protecting each new garden. They soon realized that a deer fence was essential if they wanted a real garden and not just a series of heavily defended gulags sprinkled around the property.

Once protected from the deer, they set about transforming the landscape with bold plantings linked to the wider view.

An early decision to terrace the land above the house was so successful that they continued it on the hillside below the house, creating sloped planting beds with paths winding between the levels. The planting responds to the topography and site conditions: a wet area is planted with bog plants; a sweep of daylilies blankets a particularly steep pitch. Everywhere, the planting is muscular, with large stands of grasses and shrubs interspersed with generous quantities of perennials. A wide path winds down the hillside, defining major planting areas.

The property came with a pond set on the only level piece of land below the house. Moore and Nereaux dug a second, but still felt there was something missing as they surveyed the garden tumbling down the hill and decided they needed a building on the edge of the larger pond. They designed and built a simple, shingle-roofed summerhouse that anchors the composition. As a result, in the view over the garden, there is water in the foreground that evokes the Hudson below, even when the river itself is not in sight. The scale of the planting around the ponds is particularly effective; the large clumps of grasses add the right amount of weight. The height and complexity of this midground planting around the ponds effectively hides the neighboring properties and makes a seamless transition to the river landscape. For a place with a deserved reputation as the home of a huge range of plants, this hillside garden is remarkably well balanced. It's not all intense planting: there are grassy areas and mirrored water to rest the eye, and plenty of opportunities to admire the view.

OLANA

Hudson

The painter Frederic Edwin Church first saw the dramatic hillside that would become what some call his greatest canvas in the 1840s, when he took a sketching trip on the east bank of the Hudson. At the time, he was a young student of Thomas Cole, the founder of the Hudson River School of landscape painting. Years later, when Church had become a celebrated painter and a leading figure in the Hudson River School himself, he bought a piece of property in the area, built a small house, which he called Cosy Cottage, and started a farm that would become an important element in his landscape design. In 1867, after a series of personal tragedies, Church and his wife took their family on a two-year voyage to the Middle East, visiting Beirut, Damascus, and Jerusalem. Deeply affected by the exposure to those cultures, Church jettisoned his plans to build a chateau-like home on the brow of the hill above his cottage, and instead hired the architect Calvert Vaux to help him design a Persian-inspired mansion. The resulting house, which he called Olana after a fortress treasure house in ancient Persia, took many years to complete. Dominating the landscape for miles around, the exuberant, highly ornamented silhouette of Church's Orientalist folly has become a regional landmark.

In contrast to the exotic inspiration of the house, the landscape might be seen as the culmination of a century's worth of thinking about approaches to the native American landscape. Church, a follower of Alexander von Humboldt, was a prominent figure in the intellectual life of New York. Both Olana and his city house were the site of frequent gatherings of the intellectual lights of his time, including Frederick Law Olmsted and Vaux. It is not surprising, therefore, that the landscape at Olana seems like a distillation of the ideas developed by Andrew Jackson Downing and then perfected in Central Park.

Church worked on his property continuously for the forty years he lived at Olana, and the garden is the entire designed landscape. His design for Olana included park, forest, his own *ferme ornée*, and water, always with the panoramic view in mind, a view that he painted many times. He planted thousands of trees singly and in groups, sculpting his view of the mid- and foreground, and created a ten-acre lake southeast of the house, answering the long vista of water in the distance. One of his later projects was a cutting flower garden that was accessible yet hidden from the house, so as not to interfere with the larger view. The garden, backed by a south-facing stone retaining wall, could be glimpsed as an event from a section of the carriage drive, but then receded from view in the final, heightened approach toward the house. Church took special delight in his carriage drives, meticulously composing the vistas, the turns, and the sequence of light and shadow as the roads wound through forest and field and around the lake, rising to specific lookout points where vistas had been opened up. Especially after the 1870s, when his style of painting slowly faded from fashion, the landscape became his primary canvas. He said of his work on the estate, "I can make more and better landscapes in this way than by tampering with canvas and paint in the studio."

RIVER SCHOOL FARM

Livingston

Set on a knoll on the side of Blue Hill, this 150-acre farm of rolling apple orchards lies in the viewshed of Olana, Frederic Church's estate, which is no more than two miles away as the crow flies. The views west to the Catskills are immense, and the light that goes along with this outsize vista is endlessly changing. One of the underlying ambitions of this garden is to capture and frame the view, creating some drama and interest in the foreground so that it is not obliterated by the vast sky but rather enhanced by it.

When Owen Davidson and Mark Prezorski bought the property in 2002, they cleared out the tangled overgrowth in the fields around their 1830s farmhouse, leaving a single white pine tree and several tall black locusts as foundations of their plans and opening up the expansive views. They gave the property the name River School Farm in honor of the group of painters who glorified the Hudson River landscape in the nineteenth century. The property had a stream and a large irrigation pond (they have since added another), excellent soil, and a favorable microclimate, all of which made it possible to start building gardens on seven acres of land surrounding the house. The Hudson River is only one set of hills away and a constant presence.

In the short time that Davidson and Prezorski have gardened here, they have collected a wide range of plants, including numerous varieties of gingko, dwarfs and standards as well as full-size specimens; more than fifteen varieties of magnolias; and an extensive group of witch hazels. There are more than one hundred roses that thrive here with no spraying, including an assortment of old roses, such as rose gallica and many different rugosa roses.

The evergreen and deciduous conifers in the pinetum, which they have collected in large numbers and in all shapes and sizes, give weight to the immediate landscape and help to balance it with the wide-open view. A lookout built in the orchard above the garden affords a view of the Hudson River as well as a telling bird's-eye view of the design, which reveals the importance of the collection in the construction of the garden. The tight, dense shapes of the conifers focus the eye before it travels further over the fields below and mountains beyond. Throughout River School Farm, trees and shrubs are used as others would use perennials, planted in great sweeps that shape the spaces and narrow and widen the views. Gravel paths wind through a rock garden, laid out on a gentle rise a short distance from the house. Conifers dominate the planting here too, with taller ones such as the Swiss stone pine on one side and dwarfs on the other; perennials are interspersed, mostly large swaths of blue-flowering ones such as salvia, lavender, and phlox. The path through this garden ends in a small gravel terrace with two chairs offering another vantage to contemplate the wider landscape and the turret of Olana in the distance.

TAILINGS

Germantown

W hen David Whitcomb and Robert Montgomery moved to this wooded hilltop in 1986, the splendid views that give such resonance to the garden were not apparent. Whitcomb, a gifted interior designer and gardener who died in 2001, understood the site's possibilities and chose to build the house and make the garden among the trees on the top of the long ridge. They named the property Tailings, which refers to mining residue, since it was on the site of a former iron mine operated in the 1880s by the Livingston family. As they worked on the land and began making axial cuts through the woods, a magnificent 360-degree view appeared, from the Berkshires to the Hudson River and the entire Catskill range beyond.

Whitcomb selectively culled trees, carefully shaping the views, while retaining a sense of privacy for the house, which consists of four linked pavilions of differing architectural styles gathered together in a series of follies. Glass-roofed walkways link Palladian, Greek Revival, contemporary, and postmodern wings. Cement and rusticated concrete block, used principally in the connecting walkways and entranceway, are covered with ivy, evoking an industrial ruin; the pavilions, although alluding to historical periods, look fresh and new. The question of what is old and

what is new extends to the gardens, where architectural remnants have been placed throughout the landscape. Often, the answer is both. At the top of the long driveway leading to the house are six wooden columns that used to mark a vegetable garden (now a lawn): two are nineteenth-century antiques, and the other four are copies.

The landscape, with its piercing views cut through the natural woodland, complements the architecture. Woodland paths connect a series of gardens and plantings; for the most part, the plantings create a restful environment with an emphasis on green. The choice of soft colors, such as the pale pinks of Japanese anemone or the gentle blues of Siberian iris, catmint, and Russian sage, works well with the naturalistic tone. Woodland plants, chosen for their foliage, are grouped in large numbers to best effect. Pots of blue agapanthus, the only container plantings, add an elegant touch in the summer.

The garden tempers and humanizes the glass and concrete block exterior of the house, and, at the same time, curving concrete walls shape the adjacent exterior spaces. Ivy, and occasionally variegated euonymus, clothes the concrete walls, causing them to melt into the landscape. In the notheast-facing courtyard, the relationship between the ivy-clad walls and the gravel paving is as classic and serene as any medieval cloister.

Whitcomb had a knack for combining different elements, often from disparate eras, in ways that provoke questions, encouraging the examination of long-held assumptions. Not being able to quite categorize what you see serves to sharpen the senses, which in turn increases your appreciation of the garden and ultimately of the sweeping view below.

CONRAD HANSON

Germantown

W hen Conrad Hanson started to garden here in 1999, he was inspired by the history of his house, a small-scale Italianate manor built by a prosperous farm family in the1850s, perhaps modeled on the grand river estates nearby, as well as by the old-fashioned flowers he found in the gardens, which reminded him of the plants he knew as a child in upstate New York. The modestly scaled garden grew bit by bit, as Hanson relied on his instinct and impulses, rather than on professional landscape plans. Taking a cue from what existed, he let the garden unfold naturally, further motivated by trips to local nurseries where he hunted for plants that he liked and wanted to bring home.

Complementing the classic styling of the house, the front garden is mostly green, with a burst of Casablanca lilies in the summer. It is behind the house where Hanson's garden becomes vibrant and colorful. A rectangular gravel courtyard, partially shaded by a mulberry tree, is a place to rest and view the garden. The main focus is a bed of clipped boxwood surrounding an elaborate cast-iron fountain that a friend of Hanson's found in a junk shop. Hanson has a way with planters, which successfully set the tone for the gardens in which they sit. Victorian urns, festooned with ferns and annuals, mark the paths and steps. A series of

bright blue planters, some filled with gray foliage plants, add a humorous touch to the formality of the historic property.

Beyond the courtyard, island beds in the lawn display large groups of perennials, some of which were already in the garden when Hanson arrived. What was only a clump of iris grew to an impressive iris display. A few phlox masking the septic tank were moved and divided over time to become a mass of phlox delineating the back of the garden. Two tree peonies and an herbaceous one anchored what grew into a long, serpentine peony bed. A small circle of daffodils turned into a formal box-edged circle surrounding a tall, iron *tuteur*. Throughout the beds, the small conical shapes of dwarf Alberta spruce add a touch of formality to the loose planting, which for the most part is made up of traditional favorites such as roses, daisies, coneflowers, and phlox, supplemented by annuals such as blue salvia and dahlias.

This is a garden of moments. After the daffodils planted thickly along the edge of the adjacent woods finish blooming, there is the peony moment, then the phlox moment, and of course the lily moment. Late in the season, when gardens are often spent, this one reaches the ultimate peak when the dazzling show of dahlias blooms at the same time as the sweet autumn clematis draped over four *tuteurs* in a big rectangular bed in the center of the garden.

MONTGOMERY PLACE

Annandale-On-Hudson

The charms of Montgomery Place have bewitched visitors since the mansion's creation in 1805. Andrew Jackson Downing proclaimed that it is "nowhere surpassed in America in point of location, natural beauty, or the landscape gardening charms which it exhibits," in his book *A Treatise on the Theory and Practice of Landscape Gardening*. The nearly four-hundred-acre estate still demonstrates the qualities so admired by Downing, whose ideas did much to shape an American landscape aesthetic in the nineteenth century. Montgomery Place also presents an evocative picture of two centuries of American engagement with the land, and it illustrates the important influence of women in shaping domestic landscapes.

Janet Livingston Montgomery, the Chancellor's sister, had spent her childhood at Clermont, the family estate several miles up the river, and lived near Rhinebeck after her marriage. A quarter-century after her husband, General Richard Montgomery, died at the Battle of Quebec (1775), she bought this property, which was then a working farm. She built a Federal-style mansion that she named Chateau de Montgomery to honor the memory of her husband, who was celebrated as the first hero of the Revolution. At age fifty-nine, this redoubtable woman expanded the

place, eventually running a successful orchard and seed business. Keenly interested in botany, she built a greenhouse to nurture exotic specimens sent to her from afar, but her interest in ornamental plants did not extend to the landscape, and her house was surrounded by agricultural land. However, she did site her house on a bluff, which, like Clermont, had a spectacular view of the Hudson and Catskills beyond.

She left the property to her younger brother Edward; his widow, Louise, embellished the grounds, replacing Janet's greenhouse with an ornate Gothic one, laying out walks and follies in the landscape. Louise and her daughter, Coralie Livingston Barton, were sophisticated and well traveled, and together they completed the transformation of the area around the house from working farm to pleasure grounds, although there is a still working orchard on the estate. They invited Alexander Jackson Davis, the premier architect of the day, to remodel the house, and Davis brought his great friend and collaborator Downing to guide the development of the landscape. Based on plans drawn up by Downing, Louise and Coralie added elaborate French parterres, which no longer exist. Coralie's husband, Thomas Barton, developed an arboretum on the property, with the help of Downing's advice and supplies. Downing was a nurseryman as well as a tastemaker, and by then he had become a friend. The trees at Montgomery Place remain one of its glories. Of particular note are the massive black locusts, some of them predating even Janet Montgomery.

The next great gardener at Montgomery Place was Violetta White Delafield, whose husband, General John Ross Delafield, inherited the estate in 1921. As a young woman, she was a practicing mycologist and had published her botanical drawings. A scientist at heart, perhaps ahead of her time, she did an inventory of the flora and, intensely interested in seed conservation, also commissioned a census of native plants on the property. The Delafields restored the trails and carriage drives, and pruned the old trees, replanting where necessary and adding an understory of unusual specimens such as sourwood, silverbell, and kousa dogwood. Deeply respectful of the historic landscape she had inherited, Violetta tucked a series of new garden rooms, which were fashionable in the 1920s and 1930s, into pockets to the south of the house, so they would not compete with the naturalistic style of the property. Her gardens included a rose garden, an alpine garden, a wild garden, and the celebrated green garden, with its rotunda of hemlocks enclosing the ellipse pool. A giant tulip tree overlooks the potting shed and greenhouse and the Colonial Revival herb garden, designed by her friend, Helen Page Wodell, who had created gardens for some of the finest estates in New Jersey.

The orchards and the trees remain important parts of the landscape, as do most of Violetta's gardens, which continue to flourish in their own private world. Although Montgomery Place is a large estate, its scale is personal, and the grounds, which tell the story of two hundred years of landscape history so eloquently, still express the spirits of Janet, Louise, Coralie, and Violetta.

BLITHEWOOD

Annandale-On-Hudson

I ntricately wrought without being too busy, intimate rather than grand, the garden at Blithewood manages, like all good Italian gardens, to fit into its surroundings and complement the magnificent landscape it inhabits. This formal Italianate confection, now part of the Bard College campus, is a far cry from earlier gardens in this location, which was once the site of one of the best-known American picturesque gardens. Alexander Jackson Downing considered the nineteenth-century Blithewood property, like its close neighbor Montgomery Place, as an exemplar of a thoroughly modern American landscape. A present-day visitor would concur with Downing's opinion that the "natural scenery here is nowhere surpassed." The Hudson, four miles wide at this point, is a majestic and tranquil presence, and the rolling fields that surround the mansion are still graced with mature trees, a legacy from the romantic period.

Blithewood has had a number of owners, but three families stand out in its development. The first are the Donaldsons, who bought the estate in 1835. In conjunction with Robert Donaldson's good friends, Downing and the architect A. J. Davis, the family made the estate a byword of tastefulness in the new American picturesque manner, with a Gothic Revival

house set in rolling lawns dressed with clumps of trees as well as scenic garden walks. An illustration of the estate in Downing's book *A Treatise on the Theory and Practice of Landscape Gardening* was widely disseminated.

The Bards, who purchased the estate in 1853, were interested in education and good causes. While they built a number of structures on the property, the landscape received less attention. They did, however, donate land to the nascent St. Stephen's Seminary, which eventually became Bard College. After the death of their only son, the Bards moved to Europe, rarely returning to their estate.

In 1899 the property was sold to Captain Andrew C. Zabriskie, scion of a wealthy real estate family and well-known numismatist. Taste had moved on, and the country was in the full flush of the American Renaissance. Beaux-Arts ideals of symmetry and order replaced Davis's preferences for asymmetrical buildings. In disrepair, the rustic Gothic house was torn down, and Zabriskie commissioned Francis Hoppin, an MIT and Ecole des Beaux-Arts graduate, who had worked at McKim, Mead & White, to design his new house and garden. Hoppin, known as the premier architectural renderer of his day, was working concurrently for Edith Wharton on The Mount, her house in Lenox, Massachusetts, as well as drawing up her plans for her Italian garden.

Hoppin designed a thirty-room Georgian mansion for the Zabriskies. He has been quoted as saying that gardens should be designed all of a piece with the house, and that was certainly the case at Blithewood, where the garden projects seamlessly on axis from the narrow western facade of the white house and flows down the hill in marble steps and five terraces to arrive at an enclosed Italianate garden distinguished by white marble flourishes and a small copper-roofed pavilion.

Descending from the house, the regular axial design of the neoclassical garden, which has a central walk interrupted by a pool and sundial terrace and terminating with the pavilion or summerhouse, can be enjoyed in plan, like a drawing. The walls, which are white on the exterior, are warm brick within the garden. The venerable wisteria that covers the two pergolas on either side of the pavilion is original to the garden, as are some of the roses, peonies, and iris. The boxwood-edged parterres are now filled with grasses and relaxed shrubs, and perennials such as butterfly bush and Russian sage have replaced some of the original turf and green, clipped hedges and uprights. It is possibly this softer, looser silhouette that bridges the gulf that divides the Gilded Age and a twenty-first-century college. The garden, which has none of the stiff formality associated with classical gardens but all of their restful symmetry, has become a treasured spot on campus.

AMY GOLDMAN

Rhinebeck

Amy Goldman's mixed landscape of fields, forest, ponds, orchards, and gardens sits on rolling highlands within the watershed of the Hudson River. It is in the best tradition of those seventeenth- and eighteenth-century *fermes ornées* where owners both beautified their land and pursued serious scientific causes. The two-hundred-acre property, an old dairy farm, had been known for its unproductive soil, but Goldman has spent twenty years transforming it into an unusually productive place. The main workhorse garden on the farm is the one-acre vegetable garden where Goldman, who has written books on melons, squash, and tomatoes, trials vegetables for her own projects and for Seed Savers Exchange. To give an idea of what is meant by working garden: for her book on tomatoes, she grew one thousand varieties in order to profile two hundred of the most beautiful ones. There is a strong sense of purpose and a meticulous attention to form as well as function that underlies all the gardens that Goldman has created.

Close to the late-eighteenth-century farmhouse are a series of ornamental gardens, all of them reflecting the work of a passionate gardener. The potager, surrounded by a gleaming white picket fence, is where Goldman grows individual varieties of different vegetables in isolation for seed

collection, but it is the herb garden, nestled between the isolation garden and the greenhouse, that is the centerpiece of this part of the property. Designed by Lisa Cady, an herbalist, the garden is an interpretation of the traditional cloister garth, with two intersecting paths converging in the center and dividing the space into quarters. The herb garden is an extension of Goldman's scientific interests, with more than a hundred species of herbs displayed to be satisfying aesthetically, with repeated elements, such as boxwood, echoing across the garden for rhythm and balance. Pots containing herbs are placed strategically throughout the garden, and herbs spill over the edges onto the brick paths and bluestone border.

Overlooking it all is a handsome fieldstone pergola designed by Mary Riley Smith, covered in hardy kiwi vines that produce edible fruit in the fall. In the midground below the pergola, there is a mixed border of shrubs and perennials, including roses and lilies in soft colors; a narrow, winding fieldstone path links the isolation garden on one side and the rose garden on the other. Beyond the pergola is the swimming pool, surrounded by plantings designed by Edwina von Gal. Contemporary in tone, it overlooks the long pond, which had been formed by damming up a swampy area decades before Goldman bought the property.

The adjacent Gothic-style greenhouse, which looks like a decorative accessory to the garden, is in fact the heart of the enterprise. As befits a gardener who keeps her own seed bank, Goldman starts all her seeds herself and does the pricking out and transplanting as well. She keeps careful notes on all her garden work so that she knows exactly what has succeeded and what has not, ensuring that she is ready for the start of every season.

VANDERBILT MANSION

Hyde Park

The vast formal garden complex at the Vanderbilt estate has the pomp and grandeur that might be expected from a scion of the family whose lifestyle exemplified the Gilded Age. While the scale of the ornamental flower gardens gives some idea of the family's lifestyle, Frederick William Vanderbilt's stewardship of the landscape was exemplary. Not as fond of social life as his wife, Louise, he would disappear for hours with his estate superintendent to visit his grounds, which even then were legendary. It is clear that Vanderbilt understood its historic importance and appreciated the beauty of his land.

Almost a century before Vanderbilt bought the six-hundred-acre property in 1895, it was part of a large farm owned by Samuel Bard, a well-known New York doctor who attended George Washington. Bard was interested in horticulture, and he is thought to have built greenhouses and planted the gingko tree that still graces the front lawn of the estate. In 1829 his heirs sold the property to Bard's protege and good friend Dr. David Hosack, who, in addition to being a physician, was a passionate botanist and founded New York's first botanical garden, Elgin Botanic Garden, on the site of what is now Rockefeller Center. When Hosack retired from

medicine to become a country gentleman, he was determined to make his place a botanical and horticultural showplace. In addition to building greenhouses and collecting exotic plants from all over the world, he hired a recent Belgian immigrant, André Parmentier, who was a proponent of the new romantic park style that had caught on in Europe but not yet in America. Parmentier laid out the grounds, including the broad, sloping lawn down to the river, and provided many of the trees from his nursery in Brooklyn, essentially shaping the landscape that we see today. Such was Hosack's industry, drive, and hospitality that at the time of his death six years after he bought the property, Alexander Jackson Downing already considered the estate one of the finest in the country. It was sold to John Jacob Astor for his daughter Dorothea Langdon, whose heirs eventually let it decline and sold the estate to Vanderbilt.

Frederick Vanderbilt immediately set about clearing the underbrush that had grown up and restoring the landscape, hiring McKim, Mead & White to design the vast mansion that would replace the deteriorating wooden structure that came with the property. He preserved the splendid views, drives, and trails, upgrading where he deemed necessary, and commissioned the white bridge over Crum Elbow Creek, built by W. T. Hiscox, one of the first concrete and iron bridges in the country.

Although Vanderbilt inherited the walled gardens and greenhouses that the Langdons had built, shortly after he bought the estate he commissioned noted landscape architect James L. Greenleaf to entirely redesign them in an Italianate style, rebuilding greenhouses, adding brick piers to the brick-walled enclosure, and organizing the garden into a series of descending terraces. The focal point is a loggia decorated with the statue of an odalisque in mid-dance. In 1913 Vanderbilt commissioned Philadelphia landscape architect Robert B. Cridland to design a two-tiered rose garden with a simple pool and pavilion; Cridland continued to work

on the estate's gardens until Vanderbilt's death in 1938. Louise Vanderbilt's niece, who inherited the estate, gave it to the National Park Service with the assistance of her neighbor Franklin Delano Roosevelt. Although the palm house and greenhouses are gone, the annual, perennial, and pool gardens have been rehabilitated and, since 1984, have been cared for by the Frederick William Vanderbilt Garden Association. It is a monumental task: the annual beds alone are filled with 6,500 plants, the perennial beds have 3,200, and there are more than 1,800 rosebushes.

Much has been made of the opulence and extravagance of the Vanderbilts' lifestyle, but beyond the lore about the houses, yachts, and vast wealth, Frederick Vanderbilt left a landscape that provokes a deep, universal appreciation.

HOSACK FARM

Hyde Park

If there are guiding principles in the development of the landscape at Hosack Farm, they are recovery and revelation: the recovery of a picturesque nineteenth-century landscape that had been lost to the layers of time and the revelation of the prehistoric terrain in the long, rocky ridges and tumbling rockfalls that mark this ninety-five-acre property.

Hosack Farm was once part of the neighboring Vanderbilt estate, and, in 1896, when McKim, Mead & White was working on the design of the mansion for Frederick Vanderbilt, the firm undertook the design of this fieldstone house for one of his favorite nieces. When the present owner arrived, the forest had reclaimed the open fields that once surrounded the house and most of the landscape infrastructure as well. A master plan was developed for improving the property, and a horticulturist was engaged to oversee the choice of plantings. The estate was given a new name, Hosack Farm, in honor of David Hosack, the dynamic physician and botanist who had once owned the Vanderbilt property.

A series of formal gardens with boxwood edging and a pergola based on a Lutyens design dress the house. Containers overflow with annuals, and a garden featuring different varieties of Chinese peonies provides a brilliant show in the spring. For the most part, however, efforts have been

focused on the larger landscape: uncovering the layers, eliminating the detritus of time, and patiently studying the land before deciding how to proceed. As the edge of the woodland was cleared near the house, plants started to appear: a tiny cyclamen and a few hellebores thriving under a pine tree were a signal to plant more, a few heirloom daffodils were encouraged to multiply, a rock struck while digging a flowerbed turned out to be the top of a rustic staircase leading down the ridge from the house.

The topography of the property is unusual: fingers of glacial debris with soil in between. Giant moss- and lichen-encrusted rocks are strewn throughout the property, so typical of the Hudson Valley. The forest is being opened up one tree at a time, with the aim of revealing the deeper landscape. This careful pruning and clearing has unveiled many treasures, such as a small silted-up woodland pool, which has been restored and now provides a poetic moment in the larger landscape as well as a romantic venue for skating parties.

Possibly the greatest surprise in the ongoing development of the landscape at Hosack Farm was the discovery of the bridge. Carriage drives, part of Vanderbilt's extensive network, once threaded the property. A chance sighting of the date 1905 on a low stone wall prompted a closer examination of the rubble surrounding it, which turned out to be the remains of a 20-foot-high, 120-foot-long dry stone wall bridge alongside Crum Elbow Creek that Vanderbilt had installed. Now beautifully rebuilt, it is a reminder of the old Vanderbilt estate, perfectly illustrating the value of this slow, considered approach to landscape.

BELLEFIELD

Hyde Park

In photographs of the flower garden at Bellefield taken in 1927 when the Newbold family still lived there, the spires of white foxglove show up sharply against the stone walls and hemlock hedge that surround the garden. Foxgloves have once again seeded themselves in the elegant flower beds that line the garden walls, and, even though no planting plans for the original garden exist, the spirit if not the letter of Beatrix Farrand's design lives on in this garden, which is now part of the Franklin D. Roosevelt National Historic Site.

She was still Beatrix Jones in 1912, the year of her marriage to Max Farrand, when she designed a simple, walled flower garden, surrounded by a wild garden, for her cousin Thomas Newbold, to go with his colonial-era farmhouse, newly expanded and renovated by McKim, Mead & White. She designed the garden with the view from the drawing room in mind: at its northern end, it is exactly as wide as the house, and it extends three hundred feet south from the drawing room, its axis points crisply aligned with the fenestration. Family photographs attest to the Newbolds' enjoyment of their garden, whose simplicity matches the clean lines of the house. The long, narrow, walled garden is divided into three grassed rectangles of decreasing width. The first section is enclosed in a wall of

rough-cut local stone, the second and third in hemlock hedge, both choices reflecting Farrand's sensitivity to the use of local materials. The stone walls have inverted corners, a design detail that also saved a large existing oak at the northeastern side of the garden and a maple in the southeast corner. The decrease in width of the garden forces the perspective and makes the end seem further away.

After the Newbolds' grandson gave the property to the National Park Service in the 1950s, the garden deteriorated and was covered for some time in black plastic to minimize the weeds. In 1994 a group of gardeners and neighbors set out to rescue the garden, and after four years of research and work, they hired a curator to guide the rehabilitation. As no planting plan existed, they used plans for another, similarly shaped Farrand garden as a template, the Read Garden in Harrison, New York. Starting with the Read color schemes and plant palette, as well as the many photographs of the Newbold garden, which showed a predominance of white and pastel tones, the gardeners at Bellefield developed a planting design that works for twenty-first-century aesthetics and is also historically appropriate. Brighter colors, mostly darker blues, purples, and pinks, are featured in the beds closest to the house; extending south into the garden, the lighter colors—white on the east side, a mix of cream, blush, and gray (an unusual combination particular to Farrand's borders) on the

west side—subtly extend the perspective down to the gate at the bottom of the garden. Remarkably, some plants did survive the years of neglect, most notably a number of pale-colored peonies as well as a garden stalwart, white camassia. Searches among other historic properties have turned up prized plants of varieties Farrand is known to have used, which include iris Black Prince from Thomas Jefferson's garden at Monticello and pass-along plants from other Beatrix Farrand gardens.

In such a small garden, the walls are particularly important. Farrand's trellis system is both decorative and practical: chestnut slats for the uprights (which survive) and bamboo for the horizontals (which is replaced regularly). Farrand insisted that vines be kept strictly in check, with the tracery clearly visible, so there is constant work to keep the wisteria, akebia, honeysuckle, and trumpet vine neatly within bounds.

The planting continues at Bellefield, with an eye to fine-tuning Farrand's sophisticated plant palette to the vagaries of climate, shade, and woodchucks. The gardeners have focused closely on making this garden true to Farrand's spirit, looking on the project as an homage to a great practitioner. The surprise is how fresh it all looks. Farrand's garden speaks to us just as clearly today as it did to the Newbolds and their guests a hundred years ago.

LOCUST GROVE

Poughkeepsie

The gardens and grounds at Locust Grove retain the atmosphere of a domestic landscape that has been shaped for the most part by the people who owned it, rather than by professional designers. Its most famous owner, Samuel Morse, the inventor of the telegraph, was an artist, and he lectured on landscape art to the National Academy of Design. His successors, the Young family, paid as much attention to their landscape as to the house. The Youngs left a wealth of information, including planting diaries and extensive seed lists. Morse's legacy is the broad outline of the landscape; the now-giant trees, including tulip poplars, gingko, maple, and beech; and the shaping of the estate into a vivid example of the nineteenth-century picturesque aesthetic.

Like so many estates on the east bank of the Hudson, this was once a Livingston property. Henry Livingston Jr. inherited it in 1771 and farmed here until 1828. In 1830 an Irish immigrant, John Montgomery, purchased it as a country estate, and he in turn sold it to Morse in 1847. Morse was very much part of the wider artistic community of his day, and he asked his friend Alexander Jackson Davis to draw up the plans for the Italianate villa he designed for himself and his family. Morse set about creating the landscape, shaping views, planting trees, laying out the looped driveway, and developing carriage drives linking up with

neighboring properties. He was interested in all aspects of gardening, from the large gestures to the kitchen garden; one of his passions, like many wealthy men of his day, was raising table grapes in his greenhouse.

The Young family bought the estate from Morse's sons in 1901, after they had been tenants there since 1895. Martha Young was another passionate gardener, and she was exceptionally fond of flowers and of experimenting with the newest varieties. Young laid out the long, straight flower borders, where she displayed and trialed new varieties of flowers, and she started an extensive collection of peonies that visitors still enjoy in the spring.

The landscape and garden choices made by the knowledgeable staff at Locust Grove, which opened to the public in 1979, seek to reflect the point of view of eras past while livening up the grounds for visitors. Young's long beds, now surrounded by boxwood, have been planted with lavender, rudbeckia, and hydrangea. The peonies, still laid out in large blocks, occupy pride of place, along with a fine show of iris and a seventy-five-foot-long border planting of dahlias. Where possible, old varieties are included to reflect the choices that were available to Young: seeds for a pyramidal, instead of candle-shaped, delphinium were purchased from England; only pansies with faces and whiskers are used. By the house, the circular beds and urns, which are noticeable in photographs from Morse's time, are filled with Victorian bedding plants that Morse or Young might recognize, such as coleus, colocasia, ferns, and castor beans. The small picturesque park includes an expansive heirloom vegetable garden, where volunteers maintain separate areas identified with the four different families who made Locust Grove their home.

129

DUNCAN AND JULIA BRINE

Pawling

The line between art and nature has never seemed so blurred as it is at the Brine garden. Six acres of plantings appear at first to be a most exquisite bit of natural landscape, displaying a minimal amount of human intervention—a bench here, a gravel path there, a simple bridge over a flowing stream. In fact, it has taken landscape designer Duncan Brine and his wife and partner, Julia, since 1990 to create this naturalistic garden. It has become the ultimate expression of a vision that favors native plants over foreigners and that, like nature, abhors a straight line and some other generally accepted tenets of garden design: there are no perimeter plantings, large garden rooms, or severe pruning. Above all, it is a vision that is deeply knowledgeable and sympathetic to plants' habits and needs, and uses them to tell the landscape story.

A farm gate is a reminder that the property was once part of the old Sheffield farm, a large dairy operation that flourished in the 1920s and 1930s. What little flat agricultural land remained has given way to a deliberately shaped landscape that is intensively and artfully planted. The Brines added contour; painstakingly cleared a dump area and brought in

gravel of various sizes, creating a rock garden focused on cacti; and then they cut pathways, linking different areas in the garden. The actual property lines are blurred by the long views of the borrowed landscape: the shape of the trees leads the eye to the distant hills, and an opening in the group of swamp cypress gives a glimpse of a neighbor's pond. Throughout, there are allusions to the past, such as the odd fence post or the old-fashioned English washbasins used as stools; however, no allusion is immediately obvious, and the hand that has shaped the spaces is thoroughly disguised.

When the Brines first started, they planted no more than three specimens of a single plant, often choosing something that might have grown in the location naturally. If the plants thrived, which they often did, they added more. A few river birch by the twisting stream are now a grove; a single viburnum is a viburnum glade. (The Brines grow more than thirty varieties of viburnum.) Plants are repeated in different groups throughout the garden. Although the emphasis is on natives, handsome foreigners appropriate to the landscape take their place in the composition as well: a specimen katsura is positioned to echo a line of sugar maples, winter jasmine creates a cascading thicket, and a stand of Japanese cedar repeats the form of the spruce by the house. It is all about knowing the plant and patiently observing whether it will settle in or not; success is measured in the regeneration of favorite plants, such as the swamp oak in the stream garden.

Throughout, paths serve as the narrative link. Unlike a conventional garden where you might move directly from one delineated area to another, here the transitions from one zone to another are gradual, the groves of trees, shrubs, and perennials blending into one another, the story unfolding as fast or as slowly as the plantings allow. It might intensify in a particularly tightly packed area; there might be drama where there is an exceptionally beautiful specimen, such as the larch that picks up the golden afternoon light; or there might be a pleasing allusion, as when a grouping of Giant Chinese Silver Grass echoes the existing phragmites in the marsh, or a few swamp cypress, side by side on the edge of the property, suggest the lot line, letting the imagination do the rest.

STONECROP GARDENS

Cold Spring

Since its inception, Stonecrop Gardens has been a mecca for plant lovers. Occupying sixty-three windy hilltop acres of mixed woodland and pasture in the Hudson Highlands, it features twelve acres of gardens that are planted with a dizzying number of species, each presented to its greatest advantage. A teaching garden as well as a display garden, at every turn Stonecrop offers a sense of discovery, whether in the tiny blooms of a rare alpine or the inventive combinations in the Flower Garden.

Now a series of mature plantings, Stonecrop began in the late 1950s in the empty fields around Anne and Frank Cabot's newly built weekend home. The Cabots had an interest in alpines and rock garden plants, which quickly grew to an enthusiasm, and by the mid-1960s, Stonecrop Nurseries was selling alpines and exhibiting at major flower shows. The name seemed a natural choice when they turned up more rocks than soil as they built their first perennial garden, ultimately trucking in two feet of earth for the beds. Although Stonecrop Nurseries lasted for only six years, the passion for alpines continued, and the garden is famed for its alpine and rock garden collection that includes more than five hundred species. As their collection grew, the Cabots built rectangular, raised

tufa planters and stone beds near the potting shed to display the delicate plants.

Garden-making moved on to the rocky hillside just west of the alpine area, a daunting project that was made possible when Frank Cabot found an able partner in Cono Reale, a local stonemason originally from Sicily. Together with Sara Faust, who was in charge of Stonecrop at the time, they moved in huge glacial rocks from the surrounding woods to augment the rocky ledge. Cleverly disguised beneath the Wisteria Pavilion with its romantic moon gates (designed by Franklin Faust), a concrete reservoir provides water for an artificial stream and pool, the focal point for this lyrical area of the garden. The rocky slope seems perfectly natural, with a fascinating collection of plants tucked in the interstices between the rocks.

The Flower Garden, which is close to the house, was the first garden area that the Cabots developed. It has become an ideal setting for a profusion of blooms, inspired by the English gardens that Caroline Burgess, the director of Stonecrop, knows so well. Burgess, who trained at the Royal Botanic Gardens, at Kew, and at Rosemary Verey's famous garden, Barnsley House, came to Stonecrop in 1984 and has made it her own. One of Burgess's first tasks was the renovation of the Flower Garden, which is now divided into a series of garden rooms, culminating in the Inner Sanctum, with more than twenty different garden beds separated by grass paths. In addition to annuals, perennials, and some shrubs and trees, it contains a decorative potager, guarded by a scarecrow of Gertrude

Jekyll. Each informally planted bed has a color theme, and certain plants are repeated throughout to pull it all together. As it moves through the seasons, the intensively planted garden provides a kaleidoscope of color, texture, and form.

Garden-making has continued with the creation of a lush woodland garden, and, as part of Stonecrop's mission to "demonstrate the highest standards of horticulture," the installation of a formal demonstration garden in the middle of their fields, where more than fifty plant families are displayed in systematic order beneath a 154-foot-long T-shaped pergola.

Stonecrop, which began as a private garden, opened to the public in 1992. The concept of preserving extraordinary gardens for everyone's enjoyment, which Frank Cabot pioneered at Stonecrop, led him to found the Garden Conservancy, which seeks to preserve important gardens all over the country. What distinguishes his own garden and has won it international renown is not just the ambitious scope of the garden building but the rarity and exquisite condition of Stonecrop's plants, and the sensitivity with which they are displayed.

MICHAEL SCHOELLER

Kent Falls

I n a style that could be described as rustic Italianate, Michael Schoeller has transformed the nondescript hillside surrounding his 1825 farmhouse into a formally organized series of terraces and courtyards. If the inspiration is Italian, many of the materials are indigenous, the walls made with fieldstone found on the property. The planting within these structured spaces is green and rich, with flowers billowing over tightly controlled boxwood edging. Although the gardens are elaborate, they are firmly grounded in the site, and connections to the boulder-strewn topography of the Hudson Valley abound.

Soon after Schoeller and Gary Holder bought their farmhouse, Schoeller, a fashion and garden designer, drew up a master plan for the entire two-acre property that was strictly orthogonal, with carefully placed axes and cross-axes defining the space. Then he executed it, down to the last letter. The tightly organized garden backed up on state land, affording important protection and vistas of the surrounding rocky woodlands. In creating his plan, he highlighted the venerable maple trees standing on the property, which provided welcome shade as well as an impression of maturity for the newly constructed gardens.

Schoeller began by building the fieldstone walls and terraces closest to the house and then moving outward. He painted the lattice fencing on top of the walls nearest the house a glossy white, providing a sharp contrast to the gray of the stone and the steel gray of the house. He installed a series of formal terraces and furnished them with square-cut, clipped boxwood hedges, ensuring privacy. On either side of the house, but close to the perimeter woodland, he established brighter flower and shrub gardens, including an impressive display of old-fashioned iris and peonies.

A six-foot-high fieldstone retaining wall divides the upper and lower parts of the garden. On the upper level, visually separated by the wall and a long, rustic pergola, is a stylish 45-by-75-foot potager and cutting garden. A stone doorway provides an imposing entry to the enclosed garden, which is a tour de force of pattern and shape in three dimensions. Low boxwood hedges enclose the beds, round boxwood balls repeated through the space add rhythm, and a series of rustic tuteurs, some quite complex, add height and drama. As in the gardens close to the house, the success of the design rests on the interplay of the strict geometry and the abundant plant material softening the edges. One of the elements that unifies the garden is Schoeller's use of boxwood, which can be seen throughout the property in all different sizes and shapes, including thirty-five pots of boxwood balls placed strategically as punctuation points. Despite all this structure, the garden, and the property as a whole, manages to be both animated and unpretentious, perfectly in keeping with the simple farmhouse it surrounds.

BOSCOBEL

Cold Spring

The highly polished gardens and grounds at Boscobel are an excellent match for the graceful lines of the Federal-style house. As attractive as they are, the pleasure is enhanced a thousand-fold by the prize at the end of the path: the incomparable view across Constitution Marsh to the Hudson River and the Hudson Highlands.

Surrounded by its gardens and stately trees, Boscobel has an air of genteel permanence, as though it had always been the finest house in the neighborhood, but it is actually an expertly executed reconstruction. Its original site overlooked the river in Montrose, fifteen miles south. States Dyckman, a loyalist during the American Revolution and a man of "refined taste," as his epitaph read, began the house, and the elegant residence reflects his interest in all things English. He died after only the foundation had been built, but his young widow, Elizabeth, fulfilled his vision, completing the house in 1808. It remained in the family until 1888 but then began a long decline that ended in its being slated for demolition in 1955. Recognizing the value of the house, a local historian and a group of friends stepped in to save it, with the help of *Reader's Digest* cofounder Lila Acheson Wallace, who underwrote the restoration of the house and the installation of its gardens. The house, with its distinctive swags and

flourishes, was painstakingly reassembled on a bluff overlooking the river, and the firm Innocenti & Webel, which had worked on the nearby campus for the *Reader's Digest* headquarters, was hired to transform the surrounding barren field into grounds worthy of the enterprise. Renowned for estate work, especially on Long Island, and a pictorial approach to landscape, the firm composed an unfolding series of scenes that culminates in the dramatic view.

Within three months of the dedication of the house in 1961, the grounds were finished, with huge full-grown trees planted to suggest age and permanence. Innocenti & Webel used straight lines to link the house to the main road, with an imposing allée of maple trees lining the drive to the forecourt of the house. A rectilinear apple orchard, planted in old-fashioned varieties, leads to the rose garden in the shadow of eight weeping cherries. Designed in an English wheel pattern, the brick-paved garden features more than six hundred specimens, predominantly grandifloras but including some old shrub roses. It is enclosed by a hedge of western cedar pierced on the river side by a wide opening that frames the vista. To the west of the house, Innocenti & Webel gave the view complete command, installing a sweeping oval lawn with an inviting pathway along the perimeter and a small belvedere looking out over the river.

The orangerie, sited within the orchard but not part of the original Innocenti & Webel design, serves as the centerpiece of the mansion's herb garden, tended by the Philipstown Garden Club. Thick arms of espaliered pear underplanted with lavender line the split-rail fence and the center aisle. While the herbs, flowers, and vegetables are planted for their aesthetic qualities rather than historical accuracy, the club relies on Thomas Jefferson's garden book for reference and inspiration. Inside the tiny building, orange trees, scented geraniums, and tender herbs such as lemon verbena, rosemary, and bay are wintered over until they can be moved into the garden in the spring.

Although the focal point of the fifty-acre property is the house and gardens, curving woodchipped paths lead through the adjacent woodland to an overlook with red cedar furniture, fencing, and a summerhouse, whose rustic design was based on a painted landscape on an 1803 plate from States Dyckman's dessert service.

LISBURNE GRANGE
Garrison

The garden at Lisburne Grange is remarkable for its consistent vision and subtle whimsy, the product of an exceptionally successful collaboration. Although it is often referred to as a Fletcher Steele garden, three people were responsible for the grounds that surround the nineteenth-century mansion: Samuel Sloan, the railroad magnate who purchased the farm on River Road in 1862 and sited his house on the knoll overlooking the Hudson; his daughter-in-law Katherine "Kitty" Colt Sloan, a passionate gardener and one of the founders and early presidents of the Garden Club of America; and Steele, also a stalwart of the Garden Club and a witty and imaginative landscape architect who collaborated with Kitty Sloan for almost twenty years.

Samuel Sloan, an immensely respected businessman, loved big trees, flowers, and Mrs. Sloan. He focused on preserving the large trees on the property as well as planting new ones, especially in the large, gently sloping meadows that formed the approach to the house. In addition to native maples, oak, and hemlock, he planted the now-giant gingkos, lindens, and Chinese magnolias that still enhance the property. He also installed a cutting garden on the estate so he could bring his wife roses every morning.

When Kitty Sloan took over management of the estate, she reoriented the house to create a new garden area to the south. Focusing on the north-south axis from the piazza of the house, she laid out a wide, grassy, barberry-edged terrace, and, as a central feature, she designed what became the signature element of the garden, widely published at the time: a mirror pool installed in the shade of four huge sugar maples. She intended essentially a green garden. The axis terminated with a summerhouse visible from the house, later replaced by a Chinese-style wrought-iron teahouse designed by Steele (who also recommended the hillside sloping down from the pavilion be planted with white birch and dogwood, to produce an overall white, lacy effect). Satisfied with the north-south axis of the garden, the Sloans felt they needed professional help with the east-west axis and hired Steele in 1921.

Steele immediately recognized and admired the picturesque strengths of the estate, especially the "grandeur of the now fully grown trees" and the twenty-five-acre meadow that mediated between the house and the immense northwestern vista. To the east, cedars framed a striking mountain view, but the vexing problem for the east-west axis was an old water reservoir that had been disguised as a peculiar hump. Although it was not central enough to be a focal point, it was much too large to ignore. Steele decided to make a virtue of the defect and turned the mound into a folly. Then he sent the Sloans to Europe to shop for

ruins. They returned with Tunisian pillars for the "temple on top of the mount" and a statue to anchor a new terrace to the south. Steele encouraged Kitty to plant a rock garden on its steep hillside. The main axis was reinforced with strategically placed grass steps and pillars connected with ivy garlands.

When, after much discussion, the Sloans decided they needed a swimming pool, Steele, with typical theatrical flair, designed one based on the Fountain of the Dragons at the Villa d'Este and tucked it in the hill under the western-facing terrace. Unwilling to disturb three huge maples there, however, he turned the pool slightly off the very clear garden axis, which saved the trees and afforded the swimmers a view of the meadow below and the Hudson River. A double set of stairs curve around the fountain area down to the pool terrace, backed by a set of scroll-shaped hedges, which echo the decoration of the pool.

Many successful designs are the result of collaboration; at Lisburne Grange, it was a collaboration of equals. Kitty Sloan, as her mirrored pool attests, was an exceptional designer in her own right, and both she and Steele recognized the immense value of Samuel Sloan's contributions to the earlier landscape. Fortunately, the garden remains very much as it was in the Sloans' day, a testament to the adage that three heads are better than one.

MANITOGA

Cold Spring

ussel Wright named his property Manitoga, the Algonquin word for "place of the great spirit," reflecting his deep feelings for the woodland landscape that he had rescued and shaped for more than thirty years. Friends and visitors marveled at the natural beauty of Wright's hillside with its mossy paths, ferny glades, rock groupings, dramatic waterfall, and quiet vistas, assuming that it had always looked that way. In fact, Wright had labored painstakingly, often alone or with a few weekend guests, to carve out the garden and its two miles of paths. When he bought the property in 1942, it was an unprepossessing hillside covered with an expanse of what he called "dry impenetrable woods" that had sprung up after extensive logging and quarrying operations in the nineteenth century. He cut vistas to the Hudson River, transformed a quarry into a lake with a waterfall, encouraged the moss and ferns and wildflowers, and in the end succeeded in creating a completely natural looking garden.

Wright was the premier industrial designer of his day, his name literally a household word. His dinnerware and furniture created for everyday use by ordinary people was instrumental in making the general public comfortable with modern styles. Inspired in his work by natural forms,

he brought his designer's skills to the problems presented by his wooded hillside. He started culling trees, becoming an expert in thinning the forest, moving very slowly to avoid shocking the trees, opening up views bit by bit. After studying the land, he seemed to intuit the possibilities of any site and to tease them out. He was particularly sensitive to the natural combination of mountain laurel, hemlock, and lichen-covered rocks that characterized the Hudson Highlands forest.

Built into a rocky hillside overlooking the quarry pond, Wright's house and linked studio, called Dragon Rock, are remarkably integrated into the landscape. This is one of the few places on the property where the intent of the designer is explicitly evident; in the landscape, it is invisible. To bring his family and friends out for walks, picnics, and swims, he built a network of paths, reminiscent of the carriage drives that were built in the nineteenth century. His curving paths, which are simple mulched tracks through the woods, wind their way from meadow to glade, around rocks and through forest, over velvet blankets of moss. Every scenic moment feels like an accidental discovery, but in fact they are all tightly scripted. Wright walked and thought about every inch of the property, every vista and turn of the path, judging where to open up the trail for a stand of ferns or turn the path around a particularly interesting rock composition. He studied every possibility, and in the rare cases that he added to the landscape, the intervention was as minimal as possible: a set of simple stone stairs or a felled log thrown over a stream to form a bridge. When he did augment the landscape, it was always with native plants, such as partridge berry, hepatica, lady slippers, and rattlesnake plantain— a pioneering practice for his time. In his guidebook to the property, *A Garden of Woodland Paths*, he advises landowners to look for inspiration in their woods. In Wright's own woods, the opportunity for learning from the stone, moss, and forest is especially satisfying and a lasting contribution to landscape design.

LYNDHURST

Tarrytown

The entrance drive to Lyndhurst winds gently westward through stands of mature oak, larch, birch, and beech until gradually, obliquely, the spires and towers of the mansion appear, its mellow gray stone shaded by large trees. The rolling grounds exemplify the broad trends of American landscape design in the nineteenth and early-twentieth centuries, presenting progressively the picturesque, the romantic, and the gardenesque. Ironically, the greatest influence on this quintessentially American landscape is that of a master German landscape gardener, Ferdinand Mangold, who as superintendent shaped the grounds for more than forty years.

In 1838 William Paulding, twice mayor of New York, bought a farm in Tarrytown that included Hudson River frontage, commissioning the young Alexander Jackson Davis to draw up plans and supervise the building of a Gothic Revival villa that would be called Knoll. The style, which Davis popularized, had a lack of symmetrical formality that was considered appropriate for a country setting. To go with their house, the Pauldings apparently planted the western portion of their landscape in the picturesque style, all rockery and conifers.

KATHLEEN HARROP
BOURBON
1919

BED
3

Ten years after Paulding died, his son sold the house to George Merritt, a self-made businessman who renamed the house Lyndenhurst and again hired Davis, this time to enlarge and revise the modest villa into an imposing mansion. Merritt also had aspirations for the grounds and engaged Mangold to supervise some improvements. Mangold, who had been the superintendent of grounds for the Duke of Baden after an earlier apprenticeship at a botanical garden, set about creating a park, in the best tradition of the romantic ideal of the "beautiful," with rounded groups of specimen trees dotting the lawn. Merritt, a horticultural enthusiast, also built a great onion-domed greenhouse, which at 390 feet long was one of the largest private greenhouses in the world at that time. Mangold added

beds in front of the greenhouse filled with exotic plants in the best Victorian gardenesque style.

In 1880 the infamous businessman Jay Gould, whose manipulation of the gold market had provoked "Black Friday," the first stock market crash in 1869, acquired the property and Mangold's services. Shortening the estate's name to Lyndhurst, Gould immediately bought forty thousand of the most exotic plants Mangold could find and filled the wooden greenhouse. A year later, it burned to the ground, but, undeterred, Gould replaced it with the first iron greenhouse in America, built by Lord and Burnham, based nearby in Irvington. Designed with Gothic Revival detailing to match the mansion, the vast new greenhouse, divided into fourteen sections, housed full-grown palms in the central palm house, as well as camellias, carnations, grapes, orchids, roses, and cold frames for azaleas and rhododendrons.

When Gould died in 1892, his elder daughter, Helen, took over the house and the gardens. She added colorful shrubbery and perennials to the grounds, as well as a fernery. Like her father, she took a keen interest in the greenhouses, opening them to the public every day but Sunday. Particularly fond of the orchids, she would often send them to friends for special occasions. When the rare night-blooming cereus was set to bloom, she would wake her guests, and everyone would troop down to the greenhouse to see the blossoms unfold.

In 1905, after Mangold died, Helen installed an extensive rose garden surrounded by an English-style flower border. Planted in three concentric circles surrounding a wooden gazebo, all the roses were in shades of pink. Neglected during the war years, the rose garden had almost disappeared by 1968 when the Garden Club of Irvington adopted it. Miraculously, although only a few roses had survived, the arbors and trellises were still standing, as was the iron and marble gazebo that had replaced the wooden one after Helen's sister, Anna, the duchess of Talleyrand-Périgord, inherited the estate. A new planting scheme was devised for the twenty-four beds, using the color wheel as an organizing principle and forming concentric circles around the duchess's gazebo. The garden is adjacent to the skeleton of the greenhouses, which give a hint of their old magnificence, with star magnolias and venerable gnarled Japanese maples still standing as a legacy of that time.

UNTERMYER PARK

Yonkers

Once a 171-acre showplace with a 99-room mansion and extensive, elaborate gardens, Untermyer Park now is a faint echo of what it once was, yet its grounds evoke a romantic sense of the past. Samuel Untermyer, a dynamic and successful public advocate and lawyer, was so enamored of the estate he called Greystone that he believed when he died in 1940 he was bequeathing a national treasure to succeeding generations. Despite his best intentions, a small portion of the grounds is all that remains as a Yonkers city park, and visitors walking along the mossy paths beside the stone canals can only imagine the opulent life led by the Untermyers and their guests.

Untermyer bought Greystone in 1899 from the estate of former New York governor and presidential candidate Samuel Tilden. Along with a view over the Hudson River to the New Jersey Palisades, the estate included thirteen large greenhouses, which were very important to Untermyer, an avid orchid collector and grower (he reportedly never appeared in court without a fresh orchid in his buttonhole). He enlarged the property, remodeled the house, and hired William Welles Bosworth to design the grounds. Bosworth, whose brief was to create the finest

Beaux-Arts garden in America, was already designing Kykuit for John D. Rockefeller. For Untermyer, he fashioned an elaborate network of gardens, fusing sensitivity to the views of the Hudson with Beaux-Arts principles. The result was a landscape that included wooded drives with numerous lookout points, specimen plantings, a formal Italian-style vegetable garden set on a wide terraced hillside, a dramatic staircase of one thousand steps leading to a viewing terrace over the river, and an elaborate rockery crowned by a small viewing pavilion. Untermyer was something of a showman and populist. He opened his garden to the public once a week, and each year, his gardeners bedded out five hundred thousand chrysanthemums, four hundred thousand geraniums, and three hundred thousand pansies, and he would hold flower shows at the estate like those he had seen at Hampton Court in England. Today, the sumptuous plantings are gone, as are most of the formal gardens, overtaken by the forest.

Bosworth's pièce de résistance and the best preserved part of the Untermyer estate is the Greek Garden, a one-acre formal walled garden in the Greek Revival style, where Untermyer and his wife, Minnie, once entertained lavishly. Bosworth fashioned an elaborate fantasy for the Untermyers, fusing a host of classical motifs and elements. Although diminished, this garden gives us a glimpse of the exuberance that was Greystone. The modern-day visitor walks through the doors in the crenellated entrance portico, past a curtain of beech leaves, and enters a large, rectangular space that brings to mind a Persian paradise garden. A long canal steps down the length of the garden, bisected by another canal crossing at right angles. The northern end of the garden features a dramatic pair of sphinxes, each set atop two tall columns, the work of sculptor Paul Manship (who also designed the gilded statue of Prometheus at Manhattan's Rockefeller Center). They announce a small Greek theater, where poetry readings and performances were held in Untermyer's time. The western terminus is a circular colonnade, whose tile floor is inlaid with a mosaic picture of Medusa. Stairways with intricate banisters in a Renaissance motif lead to the lower lawn, which was once the site of major events, including a famous 1923 performance by the dancer Isadora Duncan. Still eerily beautiful, the Untermyer garden continues to be the setting for public concerts and events.

ALDER MANOR

Yonkers

Toward the end of his life, copper magnate William Boyce Thompson set off on a tour of Italy with his wife, Gertrude, where he went on an extraordinary shopping spree, shipping home some three hundred tons of classical and Renaissance art to decorate the gardens of his twenty-two-acre estate. As he said to a friend, he had become "an expert on ruined things." Almost a hundred years later, vegetation is slowly taking over the garden, and the "ruined things" that Thompson brought back are crumbling away. Time has moved on, leaving behind truly a secret garden.

When Thompson, who had made a fortune on Wall Street in mining ventures, decided to buy his country property, he found a piece of land in Yonkers with a view over the Palisades, just up the road from Samuel Untermyer's estate. In 1912 he hired Carrère and Hastings, which had been responsible for the New York Public Library, to design a Beaux-Arts mansion and gardens worthy of a millionaire. The formal, classical design for the Italian Renaissance Revival house was extended by a series of stone garden terraces facing south and west toward the river. Once Carrère and Hastings had finished the general design for the grounds, Thompson took over, taking pleasure in overseeing the workmen himself and

further developing the gardens. He was a man of passionate interests, building an impressive collection of art and objets, as well as gems and minerals. He filled his greenhouses with flowers, which he entered in local flower shows, often competing against his neighbor Untermyer.

The limestone mansion still stands and has become the headquarters for an Irish cultural heritage organization, but only a fragment of the gardens remains. The underground cistern that once collected rainwater from the roof of the house for the fountains and pools is now dry. Outside, under the shade of four huge gingko trees that are set in the corners of what was once a small reflecting pool, gnarled yews and old-fashioned rhododendron have grown the size of small trees; everywhere, vines have found their way through cracks in the masonry, covering the brick and concrete walls. Thompson's European trophies—the columned temple, statues, fountains, wellheads, and architectural fragments, including the entire facade of a church—stand in the tangle of foliage, silent reminders of a grand past.

Thompson's interest in gardens went beyond his own property. Convinced that scientists could discover plants that would alleviate world hunger, he founded the Boyce Thompson Institute for Plant Research, originally housed across the street from his residence and now part of Cornell University, and the Boyce Thompson Southwest Arboretum near Phoenix, Arizona, to study plants from deserts all over the world. His famed gem collection, once displayed in specially designed rooms in the basement of his mansion, is now on view for all to see at the American Museum of Natural History in New York.

KYKUIT

Pocantico Hills

The classically inspired gardens at Kykuit are considered to be among the finest examples of their era. They are still, a hundred years later, grand and impeccably maintained, and they still have the capacity to inspire and surprise.

John D. Rockefeller did not intend to create the finest Italianate gardens in America. He was aiming for something simpler, but the task of overseeing the construction of the house and grounds was given to his son, John D. Rockefeller Jr., and the younger Rockefeller had a loftier conception of what the estate of the country's richest man should look like. Deeply sensitive to art and anxious to make Kykuit something exceptional, Rockefeller Jr. turned to a young Beaux-Arts-trained architect, William Welles Bosworth, who was sympathetic to his aspirations and had the technical training and education to accomplish his goals. The gardens, which took over seven years to make and were more or less finished by 1915, exceeded the original budget of $30,000 by over a million dollars. In their scope and execution, they far outshine the house, whose architecture was the consequence of a group of disparate architects working for an exacting client.

The strong bond between Bosworth and the younger Rockefeller resulted in a unified vision for the gardens. Although they did not undertake the work from a detailed master plan, each element was carefully conceived as part of the grand design. The topography of the site as described by Bosworth was a clamshell with a very small flat space at the top, looking out on a large view. Bosworth chose an Italian vocabulary, with its emphasis on axes, cross-axes, and terracing, which was well suited to working with the view and handling the steep slopes.

In traditional Italian gardens, the main axis would run from the entrance through the house out into the landscape, but Bosworth put the main garden axis south of the house, leaving the views through the house and western terrace unobstructed. The house commands the view (in Dutch, Kykuit means "lookout"), but the garden uses only glimpses of it. He then composed a complex series of interlocking gardens and terraces of differing moods and styles, full of surprise and lighthearted touches. The garden invites movement: stairways set to the side make it necessary to walk through one garden to reach the next; an impressive allée of pleached lindens line the north-south axis; the hedge in the lower terrace has been shaped in a wave, echoing the curves of the swimming pools on the lower terrace.

John D. Rockefeller planned to use the house only in the spring and fall, so although much of the garden architecture is created with evergreens, the flourishes are spring flowering trees such as dogwood and cherries, and plants that look spectacular in the fall, such as Japanese maple. The extensive use of exquisitely pruned wisteria, which first appears in perfectly straight columns on the entrance facade of the house

and reappears at numerous points on walls and pergolas, subtly links different elements of the gardens. The terraces immediately adjacent to the house are formal, with clipped shrubs and grass and hard-paved walkways; the gardens on the lower terraces are more informal. In places, the hard paving gives way to gravel, and geometry gives way to grottos, rock work, woodland plantings, and an Asian-inflected brook garden. Water and fountains, so critical to Italian gardens, are also central to the conception here, starting with the thirty-foot statue of Oceanus (father of the river gods in Roman mythology) that Bosworth placed in the forecourt; progressing through the countless fountains, watercourses, and pools that furnish the gardens; and culminating in the view of the mighty river.

Ironically, while the younger Rockefeller and Bosworth both loathed modern art, Kykuit is now home to one of the country's great collections of modern sculpture, and it is sited throughout their ode to classical art and values. While Rockefeller Jr. was focused on traditional art and culture, his wife, Abby, developed a strong interest in modern art and became one of the founders of the Museum of Modern Art. Their son, Nelson A. Rockefeller, governor of New York and vice president of the United States, was a voracious collector of modern art who had a special affinity for sculpture. He lived at Kykuit after his father's death and installed his art throughout the grounds. Works by Aristide Maillol, Gaston Lachaise, Louise Nevelson, David Smith, Pablo Picasso, and Constantin Brancusi, among many others, are prominently displayed throughout the gardens. Nelson Rockefeller himself sited the pieces, and the juxtaposition of the modern works with the classically inspired statues gives the grounds at Kykuit a unique and surprisingly contemporary tone.

GARDENS OPEN TO THE PUBLIC

CLERMONT STATE HISTORIC SITE

One Clermont Avenue
Germantown, New York 12526
www.friendsofclermont.org

BELLEFIELD

4097 Albany Post Road
Hyde Park, New York 12538
www.beatrixfarrandgarden.org

BOSCOBEL HOUSE AND GARDENS

1601 Route 9D
Garrison, New York 10524
www.boscobel.org

KYKUIT

Visitor Center
381 North Broadway
Sleepy Hollow, New York 10591
www.hudsonvalley.org

LOCUST GROVE

2683 South Road
Poughkeepsie, New York 12601
www.lgny.org

LYNDHURST

635 South Broadway
Tarrytown, New York 10591
www.lyndhurst.org

MANITOGA

The Russel Wright Design Center
584 Route 9D
Garrison, New York 10524
www.russelwrightcenter.org

MONTGOMERY PLACE

River Road off Route 9G
Annandale-on-Hudson, New York 12505
www.historichudsonvalley.org

OLANA

5720 Route 9G
Hudson, New York 12534
www.olana.org

PHILIPSBURG MANOR

381 North Broadway
Sleepy Hollow, New York 10591
www.hudsonvalley.org

STONECROP GARDENS

81 Stonecrop Lane
Cold Spring, New York 10516
www.stonecrop.org

UNTERMYER PARK

285 Nepperhan Avenue
Yonkers, New York 10701
www.cityofyonkers.com

VANDERBILT MANSION

4097 Albany Post Road
Hyde Park, New York 12538
www.nps.gov/vama

WILDERSTEIN

330 Morton Road
Rhinebeck, New York 12572
www.wilderstein.org

ACKNOWLEDGMENTS

This book is dedicated to Edith and Ernest Gross, whose constant support and cheerful encouragement has been indispensable to the successful completion of this project.

We'd like to thank all the people who let us invade their landscapes for days at a time and at odd hours in order to make these photographs. We deeply appreciate the homeowners and museum curators who gave us their time and let us share their spaces with the public in this book. Our regard for what it takes to make and keep a garden has grown immensely in the process.

We also want to thank our exemplary editor Elizabeth White for the tremendous care she took with all aspects of this book. And thanks to Andrea Monfried at Monacelli for her enthusiasm for our book idea and for bringing it to the printed page.

Much gratitude to Abigail Sturges for the exceptionally beautiful book design.

And special thanks to Susan Lowry and Nancy Berner for their illuminating text. It was no mean feat to distill the rich history of the Hudson Valley into its essence.

We've enjoyed working with you all.

Steve Gross and Susan Daley

Our great thanks to Sue Daley and Steve Gross, who welcomed us so generously to the partnership and whose photographs inspired us throughout. We are deeply grateful to our editor, Elizabeth White, for her confidence in us and for her steady hand. Heartfelt thanks to Anne Cleves Symmes for steering us toward this project.

We owe a huge debt of gratitude to the gardeners, who were unfailingly courteous and patient with us, enthusiastically sharing their gardens and their stories, no matter the weather. As well, we would like to convey our profound appreciation to the advisers, curators and stewards of the historic gardens: Cathryn Anders, Ray Armater, Caroline Burgess, August J. Cambria, Margaret Davidson, Kjirsten Gustavson, Bessina Harrar, Kathleen Eagen Johnson, Peter Johnson, Kathrine H. Kerin, Jane Lehmuller, Clare Levy, Barbara Licis, Martha McConaghy, Amy Parrella, Judith Pavelock, Anthony Pellegrino, Mark Prezorski, Rita Riehle, Felicia Saunders, Tim Steinhoff, Anne Cleves Symmes, Joan Vogt, Miriam Wagner, Katy Moss Warner. Special thanks to all those who read the text and answered our many questions.

Susan Lowry and Nancy Berner

Copyright © 2010 The Monacelli Press,
a division of Random House, Inc.
Photographs © 2010 Steve Gross and Susan Daley
Text © 2010 Susan Lowry and Nancy Berner

Published in the United States by
The Monacelli Press, a division of
Random House, New York.

The Monacelli Press and the M design
are registered trademarks of
Random House, Inc.

Library of Congress Cataloging-in-Publication Data

Gross, Steve.
  Gardens of the Hudson Valley / photographs by Steve Gross
and Susan Daley ; text by Nancy M. Berner and Susan Lowry ;
foreword by Gregory Long.
     p. cm.
 ISBN 978-1-58093-277-6
 1. Gardens--Hudson River Valley (N.Y. and N.J.)—Pictorial
works. 2. Gardens—Hudson River Valley (N.Y. and N.J.)—Guide-
books. I. Daley, Susan, 1953- II. Berner, Nancy, 1950- III. Lowry,
Susan, 1951- IV. Title.
 SB466.U65H834 2010
 712.09747'3--dc22
                              2010010466
Designed by Abigail Sturges

Printed in China

www.monacellipress.com

10 9 8 7 6 5 4 3 2 1